Mental Toughness and Self-Discipline:

Ultimate Guide How to Develop Your Mind

Table of Contents

Mental Toughness and Self-Discipline: 1

   Ultimate Guide How to Develop Your Mind 1

Introduction 4

Chapter 1 – The Quicker Five Stages 5

   Be Grateful 5

   Never Accept Your Death..5

   One Goal 6

   Don't Think About Weakness..7

   One For All. All For One...7

Chapter 2 – Explore Your Dark Side 9

   List The Things You Do 9

   List The Things You Want To Do...9

   Time to Delve 9

   Sharing Is Caring 11

Chapter 3 – Test Your Limits 13

   Add an Extra 10 Degrees 13

   Just a Few More..14

   If You Can't Do That Then Do This 15

Chapter 4 – Play The Hardest Level 17

   Timed Sudoku 17

   How it plays in your life? 17

   Speed Tetris or Chess 18

   How it plays in your life? 18

   Playing Against Yourself in Any Game 19

   How it plays in your life? 19

Chapter 5 – Don't Ignore, Find Out Why...................................21

Conclusion 23

Introduction

Welcome to Navy SEAL Mental Toughness and Self-Discipline: A Guide to Developing an Unbeatable Mind, a book designed to help you fortify your mind for any situation, from the mundane to the extreme. This book covers the finer aspects of Navy SEAL training to increase the strength of your mind not only in defense and strength, but also in timed stressed critical thinking which can mean the difference between life and death. This book will give you some life-lasting training and daily practices to train your mind. Let's Begin.

Chapter 1 – The Quicker Five Stages

Your mind is a scary beast with many examples of people pulling off extraordinary acts without ever having done so before. However, if you want to pull of such miracles on a regular basis, like being the reason your family survives because you were to persistent to die, then you need to get five things down in a quick succession.

Be Grateful

There are many beliefs and theories about what will happen to us when we die, but we're not dead yet. The first mental hurdle is being grateful for your pain and this is something that is literally beat into each member the Navy Seals. You need to be happy that you can experience pain because pain means you are alive to struggle even more.

This part is the hardest because your mind wants to coddle the pain and it wants to go to the darkest regions of your mind when it receives pain, but you have to be grateful for it or it will rule you. When you see an animal get hurt, they may yelp but they completely ignore it in their fight to survive. They already understand the importance of throwing away the hold that pain can take over you.

Never Accept Your Death

People think this one is easy as they already do it in normal environments or people think this is completely insane to do, but they are not in a survival situation. When you are alone with nothing but enemies around you, human or animal, the first thing that will get you killed is to accept your death. Once you accept that you will die, before you know there's no other way out, you resign yourself to lowering the frantic search for ways out of your situation.

You do not hear many survival stories of people accepting death as the fight through difficult situations. You hear of them thinking they would most likely die, but they don't accept it. When you accept something, you release any concentrated thought that your mind has on that issue, which lowers the likelihood you will notice an out in the last minute.

One Goal

Don't do this and this and this as it will get you killed. Navy Seals have directives and plans set forth by situations and whoever might be commanding them. In the field, you won't hear about what they will do about the next directive. They focus on one simple to grasp task at a time and use the plan to keep track of what they need to do overall. This is because they are unknowingly taught to do this in boot camp. Just make it through the tear gas. Just make it through this rigid course. Just survive in this woods with nothing but your gear and the environment. They are given one task to do and focus all of their attention on that singular, maybe multi-part, task.

The reason for this is that it is more efficient to quantify the issue at hand when you have smaller tasks to deal with. The more you pile on what you have to do the more your mind will get lost in everything you have to do. Just focus on one thing and get that one thing done before moving on to the next thing. Another aspect of why they do it like this is that the mission plan may change in the middle of a battlefield due to a specific situation. Planning for a situation that is not currently happening uses more resources than if you were to just deal with situations as they come. You don't plan for retirement if you're in a situation where you have no money. Instead, you focus on one task; make more money.

Don't Think About Weakness

This is another difficult one that a lot of people have a hard time believing they will have a hard time with. When a situation arises, people think about what they are being *weak* for. I can't get a job because no one is hiring. I can't say this because then they will react like this and I can't handle this. I know it may be corny but there's a can in the cannot and that's what you need to focus on. Focusing on what you cannot do will only ever lead to more things you cannot do, but focusing on things you can do will also lead to things you can also do.

The reason for this is that a Navy Seal has to deal with stressful situations and react to them quickly. I can hide in the shade from the enemy. I can eliminate this one man without raising suspicion. I can hold my breath for up to n seconds. There's are things they can do and they utilize them, but a Navy Seal that consistently thinks of what they can't do won't be a trusted person when their other teammates need someone to rely on. Negative thoughts will make a Navy Seal have an unsteady hand, a dulled mind, and an extremely closed mind.

One For All. All For One.

I am well aware this is a famous cheese ball line from one of the most renowned books in history, but Navy Seals invest heavily in this. If you are alone, then you need to accept that there will be no one to help you *at that time*. If you are with others, then you need to accept that you cannot do everything yourself and that doing so, or trying to do so, will likely get you and whomever you are with in a worse situation. If you are dealing with emotional baggage, share it, no matter how embarrassing as it may be.

Humans are a social species, which means that we perform better when we communicate with others. The less we communicate, the less we function as a group and this can lead to a death.

Chapter 2 – Explore Your Dark Side

Do not take this as advice to kill or violate someone. This is simply to convey that you need to talk about the things you do, the things you want to do, and why you want to do them.

List The Things You Do

Take a piece of paper and begin writing all the things that you do on a daily basis. Then write all the things that you have done in the past with as much detail as possible. It's important to just remember them off the top of your head. This list may not be completely accurate, but you just need a large list.

List The Things You Want To Do

We all have hopes and dreams as to what we want to do, but we're talking about immediate actions. For instance, if you want to develop a game then what you would list what your first action would be to start developing the game. This is the beginning of the overall process.

Time to Delve

This is going to be your first step in a long life of practice as this list will change over time. Go through each item on the list and write down why you want or wanted to handle the situation exactly likely that. You will experience very important moments that you want to pay attention to. These moments are when you feel forced when you are explaining it.

The reason why you are feeling this is because your brain doesn't like to be questions. It makes quick judgements and when those judgments are questioned, it attempts to hide its reasoning so don't feel bad if this is extremely difficult at first. The importance of doing this is that it will help fine tune your decisions.

This is a common practice in psychology to bare down on personal issues that are causing discomforts in the lives of their patients. Having said that, this type of practice is for when you are attempting to strengthen the mind and many military personnel have to do this but it is known by a different name; Battle Tactics. In war, there is ample opportunity to see where battles of the past went wrong and why they went wrong. There are large swathes of case studies performed on tactics of the past to better improve the tactics. This is what captains and commanders have to do in order to improve on their tactics, but nothing relates to the real thing which is why more experience on the battlefield tends to translate into promotions faster.

When they are on the battlefield they have to think quick off their feet and plan according to the situation. There are losses and wins, which is where they get the experience they need. Most of the successful ones do have to review their actions in situations and think over why something succeeded or something failed. This allows them to refine their choices into a specific set of options that will lead to greater success in battle. This is a very common practice in the military and this is also how you will practice what you have done and plan to do.

By simply reviewing what you did and why you did it, you can better choose what you should do in the future that will not only lead to success, but also be confident in your choices. That is the true goal of this practice because doubt causes a lot of issues, both in battle and in your daily life. Doubt can cause anxiety, worry, and even bodily harm. Meanwhile, having confidence in your actions has shown to have benefits in too many areas to list such as relief from disorders, better health, and even increased longevity provided you are confident and it doesn't result in an accidental death.

Sharing Is Caring

If you have any family or close friends, you should share this with them. This is extremely important because it not only gets you used to being questioned but it also gives you a second point of view. You are only one person and you will make mistakes, which means that when you make mistakes then you need someone to help you if it's too much for you.

The first property you acquiring when you share this with trusted individuals is the ability to take criticism. If you are a strong headed person who argues with anyone who disagrees with you, then this step will be that much harder to take on. Being able to take criticism is very important when you are trying to build your mental toughness because while your friends and family may hold back, the world will almost never give you the same courtesy. Just take a look at the comment section underneath a YouTube video that has a biased opinion on a controversial topics and you will see the loads of people who have no issue giving out harsh words and criticism.

In a business situation, such criticism is absolutely vital in making sure a business thrives. The customer is where the money is and when customers list out problems, the owners of the business almost always tries to focus on those areas to improve their service. This results in a consumer base that won't readily leave you, as we see with many Apple owners.

The second property that it gives you is a different perspective other than your own. This has some obvious benefits, but there's one particular benefit that will be useful to you throughout your entire life. Once you hear a lot coming from a certain perspective, your brain develops a pattern of recognizing when that perspective could be useful in situations. Examples of this are numerous when you first start out as an adult as the most common thing a young adult does in a difficult situation is compare their actions against what their parents might do. This is because the adult knows that their parent's decisions have worked in the past and when they come to a decision of their own that closely matches a perspective they've had to nearly their entire life then they can see the situation from their own perspective and their parents. Being able to see from more than one perspective will lead to a much tougher mind that can't be broken easily.

Chapter 3 – Test Your Limits

This is not to say that you need to set the bar too far to reach, but rather that you need to push yourself a little bit each time you find yourself doing an everyday challenge.

Add an Extra 10 Degrees

The most common method that any Navy SEAL uses in combat training to fortify their mind is to add an extra ten degrees to whatever activity they may be doing. With trips taking them to the middle of a desert or to the middle of a tundra, they need to be prepared to handle any type of temperature that there body is given. Therefore, utilizing the air conditioning in your house to either raise the temperature by 10 degrees or lower it by 10 degrees helps strengthen the mind against different temperatures.

The Navy SEAL's methods are a bit different when it comes to this and a tad bit more extreme, but they also have ready access to medical doctors that will remedy any hypothermia or dehydration issues. This allows them to force the soldiers to work at night pulling boats out of a freezing water that would cause the average man to stop moving out of sheer cold. You don't have this ready access, so taking it slow and getting your body ready to the temperature difference is key to not have a mountain of medical bills.

This is done for another reason beyond the obvious reason of dealing with difficult environments. When you sweat, activities become a lot more difficult to perform and even harder to complete. When you are immensely cold, your body wants heat more than anything and, in both situations, your body wants to stop and rest. Forcing your body to deal with this type of temperature difference will make difficult activities easier to handle. While the primary goal is to make it easier on soldiers to deal with an environment that changes temperature, it also helps them deal with the effects that occur when their body is overworked.

Just a Few More

To help push you to your limits, you should also make a goal and not only finish that goal but also move a little bit past that goal. As an example, if you have a daily running area where you have a set distance of where you run then you should go the distance to reach your goal and then run for a small bit more before turning around. The same is true of any other type of exercise that you do, including weight lifting. If you crunch around a hundred something pounds a day then you can either add a very small amount of weight more each time or go a few more times in your repetitions.

The obvious reason for this is that you get more muscle out of it by continuously pushing your body over your max. The only difference is that the Navy SEALs are a bit more extreme, as in if they want to run then they go to their max and then add a few more miles rather than steps. You can do this, but just remember that they have medical staff on hand if something goes wrong while you do not.

The less obvious reason that they do this is that it gets the body into a routine habit of doing more than is required. The military wants this out of its soldiers because that means they have the right to have a strong confidence their soldiers will easily pull through on a task. However, a soldier is only as good as their training, which means that if they only ever do what is required then it is likely that they won't ever improve on themselves. Improving on yourself leads to more success in dialogues, training, and business. Instead of being angry or annoyed when you have to do something, your body will instinctively look at the goal as very small as it is used to going past that goal routinely.

If You Can't Do That Then Do This

This is another technique to continuously improve on yourself. The difference is that you are always improving something else if you are not improving what you previously wanted to improve. The idea behind this is two-fold in that not only is it intended to continuously improve on yourself but that you treat your body as a whole.

The exercise is rather simple in practice, but difficult to maintain. An example of the practice is "If I can't do twenty-five pushups, then I will do fifty sit ups. If I can't do fifty sit ups, then I will run one mile." Then, you continue this pattern until you can actually do one of the exercises you had planned to initially do. The reason this is difficult to maintain is that if you can't complete one of the tasks, then you are likely to do this for hours on end.

A lot of the issue with health currently is that the average person treats it as parts on a body rather than interlocking parts on a body. This means that when they hurt their arm, they are most likely to think that something is wrong with their arm than the rest of their body. This is an issue because, just like when you become sick, health is usually dealing with issues from the whole of the body. Unless you specifically did something that hurt that part of the body, your arm could be in pain because of your spine, because of your shoulder, or even because of your heart.

By constantly finding different areas to improve upon when you can no longer improve a certain section, you are continuously improving the strength of your entire body. This carries over into how you handle situations in real life since you can usually treat a business the same way as a body. "If I can't raise efficiency in this department by ten percent, then I will decrease marketing expenditures in this department by ten percent." This works great for business if you set reasonable goals and it means your business will constantly improve. It also helps you focus on one goal at a time rather than focusing on everything at once.

Chapter 4 – Play The Hardest Level

There is a well defined reason why soldiers will often be playing the more difficult version of something. More specifically, they will play something that has an intense reaction time, multiple situations, and a military style playthrough. In this section, we'll go over a few games and why they should be played to increase your mental toughness.

Timed Sudoku

If you hate Sudoku then you will hate Timed Sudoku even more but it is vitally important that you not only play this game but get good at it. Sudoku forces you to keep your mind on all the interchangeable spots of a Sudoku board. The time constraint intensifies the strain on your mind, which means that it will literally change how your mind thinks. Sudoku naturally increases your ability to think more efficiently and solve hard problems. People who play this game often can find themselves playing a board of twenty-five or more while the average person can barely handle just nine. Adding a time limit on it will drastically force your brain to become more tactical and think in more complex patterns than before.

How it plays in your life?

In a survival situation, critical thinking is how you will survive and even worse are the times when you have little to no time in order to think clearly. This is where timed critical thinking strategies come into play and how playing such a game will save you. Your brain keeps patterns that it can use, which means that when you need to apply timed critical thinking then the same pattern that you developed by playing a Timed Sudoku game repeatedly will be used in that situation. There are games, like racing and others, that have saved lives in such situations. A ten year old child was able to save his baby brother and grandma from a car accident by being able to "take over the wheel" and using his knowledge from Mario Kart to do so. Being able to critically think and apply a usable pattern to solve a situation is vital in survival, both long-term and immediate.

Speed Tetris or Chess

This is another one that forces your brain to change because it is timed but in a different way. Tetris and Chess are both about strategy and connective reasoning, which means you not only have to think about which pieces will fit other pieces but also determine the best course of actions with the current given hands. Doing this by itself is difficult and it becomes exponentially more difficult when the activity is timed.

How it plays in your life?

Once again, this comes down to survival but more so when have to handle a group. Let's say that you are surrounded by a bunch of ignorant civilians who don't know what to do. What do you do? If you try to answer this question now, then you need some practice in critical thinking as you shouldn't have an answer but more questions. If you have more questions, then you have a good sense of critical thinking. However, this doesn't mean you should slack because better critical thinking skills means more long-term survival.

Playing Against Yourself in Any Game

This is another one that is truly difficult if played correctly and it is a great way to look deeper inside of yourself. This type of play style doesn't make sense to the average person, yet you will see this commonly among leaders in nearly every militia. That is because of one question: how do you conquer an enemy that knows every move you make? That is why playing this game correctly makes the game truly difficult. The more you are able to predict your own moves, the quicker you will be able to adapt to those moves. The first few games will seem easy and that's because you are not playing it correctly. Instead, you are planning moves to your own moves before you take a move. Take the time and truly try to beat yourself from both sides.

How it plays in your life?

This last one does quite a number of things to you and it doesn't become clear that it did this until you get used to it. At first, you will see causation to actions you take and it will seem odd to you. Then you will notice patterns in how people interact with you and you will feel detached from the situation. The last change is that you will be able to predict the average person's reaction to your action and plan accordingly. Hollywood and movie makers make this ability seem like you need a high level of intelligence, but what you really need is the ability to analyze the actions of others.

This only starts when you start to analyze your own actions in a game-like match, which translates to life only, in life, the opponent doesn't know your moves and you don't know your opponents moves. That's when your brain kicks in because you are used to knowing the other person's moves. Your brain will look at every crook and cranny of the "opponent" to see what will work and what won't work. You begin to notice that people have common patterns of actions, common areas of issue, and you will feel what the business world calls Risk Probability Statistics. Risk Probability Statistics is broken up into three parts; How much risk is there? How probable is the success of the action? Finally, statistics just means that it is quantifiable with numbers or measurements.

With the ability to feel Risk Probability, you will take advantage of the best course of action based on probable success and not even realize it. This is where you see individuals from the Navy Seals take actions that seem like they are against their own good but somehow manage to turn a situation around because of that actions. That is because only those who also feel Risk Probability will have a more successful time in beating those who are like themselves.

Chapter 5 – Don't Ignore, Find Out Why

This is the last step and it is the most difficult part of the whole process. On a daily basis, we do things without actually thinking about what we do. The problem is that we don't handle extreme situations very well, but a common problem that most people see in movies and other examples of extreme situations is that the soldier will almost always try to find out why something is being done.

This practice comes from a PhD background, as in it teaches you how to learn. If you want a strong mental attitude and to be able to handle situations the average person cannot, then you need to know the why of practically everything. If you know why are person might be angry with you then you might be able to diffuse the situation without violence. This is a key aspect in the training section of a Navy SEAL as they are taught there is more than one way to tackle a solution and the most peaceful way is often the most beneficial. If you are trying to be covert then going through the air duct, rather than putting a bullet in the first combatant you see, will hide your presence within the system longer. The leader must ask "Why do I need to kill them?" before ever letting a single bullet fly.

This will have several benefits in your life but, mostly, they will deal with efficiency or monetary savings. Unless you are dealing with a stressful combat situation, like an actual combat situation or laser tag, then this last step will mostly just help you save time and money. A Navy SEAL is quick and efficient, but they only become this way after they begin to recognize elements that will take more time with much less profit for taking that time.

Let's first look at a small example; making Rice Krispy Bars. A box of Rice Krispies is usually underneath $10 but you don't get much for it (maybe 6-8 bars). Meanwhile, you also can make your own with a bag of marshmallows, some oil, and a box of generic Rice Krispies for underneath $10. Here's where the "why" comes in; why should you make your own? It's cheaper with more quantity. It has less preservatives and you can add more ingredients if you want to. You can switch out the materials to be healthy.

Let's now look at a real useful example; marketing yourself or having someone else market for you. Why would you have someone market for you? They know what they're doing or at least more so than you. They also know the best routes to take to best advertise or at least more so than you know. If they do this as a business then they likely have more connections in the business than you do. Why market something yourself? Once you learn, you don't even have to rely on another marketer to do it or you know when a marketer is jipping you in money. The marketer is likely going to cost a lot of money as you are paying for them to market for you and also paying them to work.

Therefore, the benefit of having someone else doing it is that you don't have to worry about doing it yourself. The benefit of doing it yourself is that you don't have to pay someone else to do it and when you do decide to have someone else do it, you can make sure you are getting the best deal for the money that you have. A Navy SEAL would likely try to learn it for themselves for this very reason with only a factor of time consumption stopping them. Understanding the "why" of any situation and further questioning the logic behind it will get you to your solution much faster.

Conclusion

Welcome to the end of this book and this is where we part ways. We've covered several different areas of where you can improve the way you think in order to strengthen your mind.

While this may be the end of this book, this is not all there is to learn. After all, such books like The Art of War, still sit on digital shelves just waiting to divulge more information to you. Until next time, good luck and the only easy day was yesterday.

OR Go to this URL

http://zbit.ly/1WBb1Ek